P9-CMY-906

RONALD SEARLE

More Cats

THE STEPHEN GREENE PRESS

For Mô

The drawings on pages 23 & 25 were originally designed as covers for the New Yorker *magazine*

First published in 1975 by Dobson Books Ltd, 80 Kensington Church Street, London W8 4BZ, England. This first American Edition has been produced in Great Britain. It is published in 1976 in the United States of America by The Stephen Greene Press, Brattleboro, Vermont 05301.

Library of Congress Catalog Card Number: 75-24952
ISBN 0-8289-0264-X

The Long March

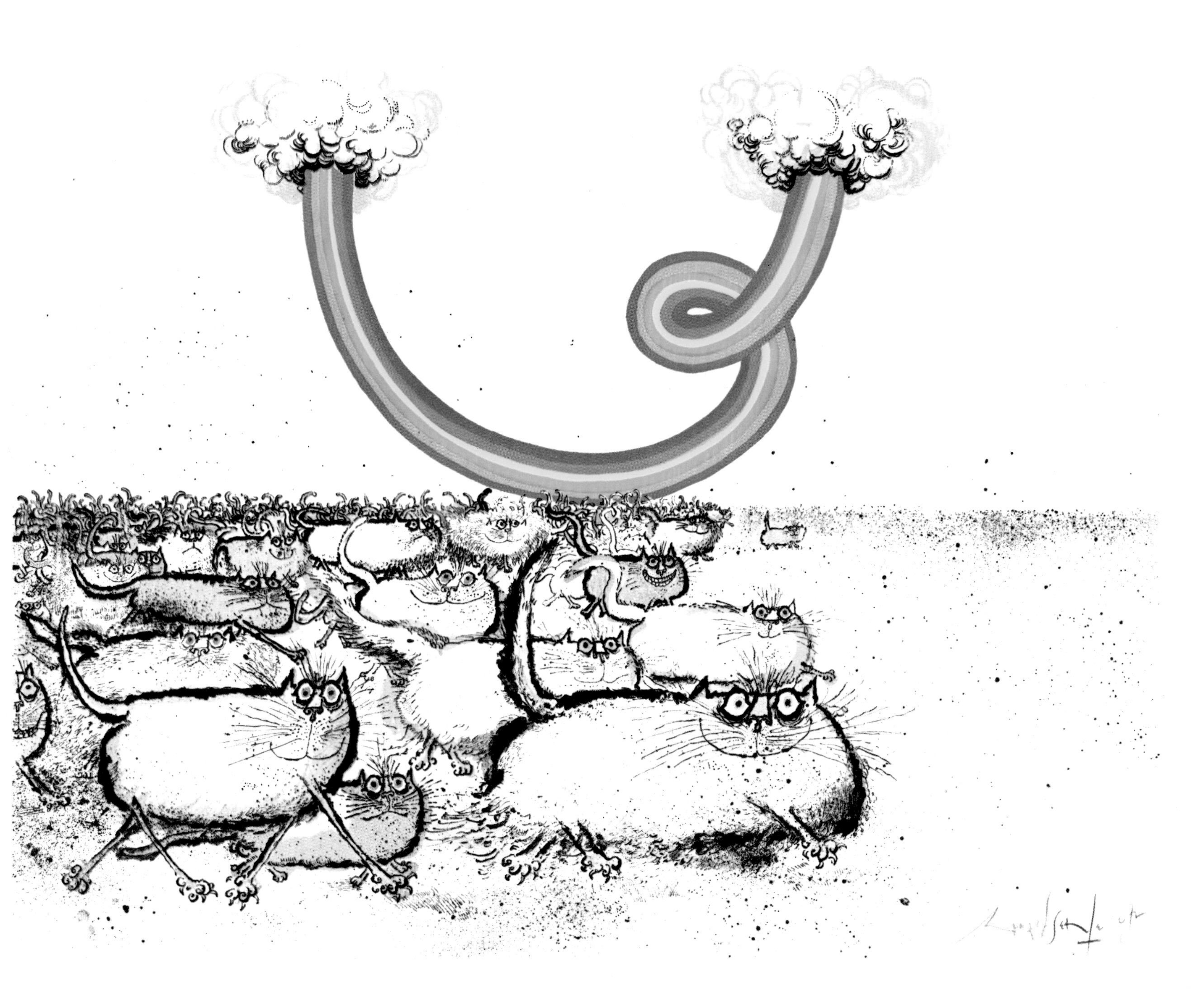

Idyll

Nobody loves me . . .

Catalogue

The morning after the night before

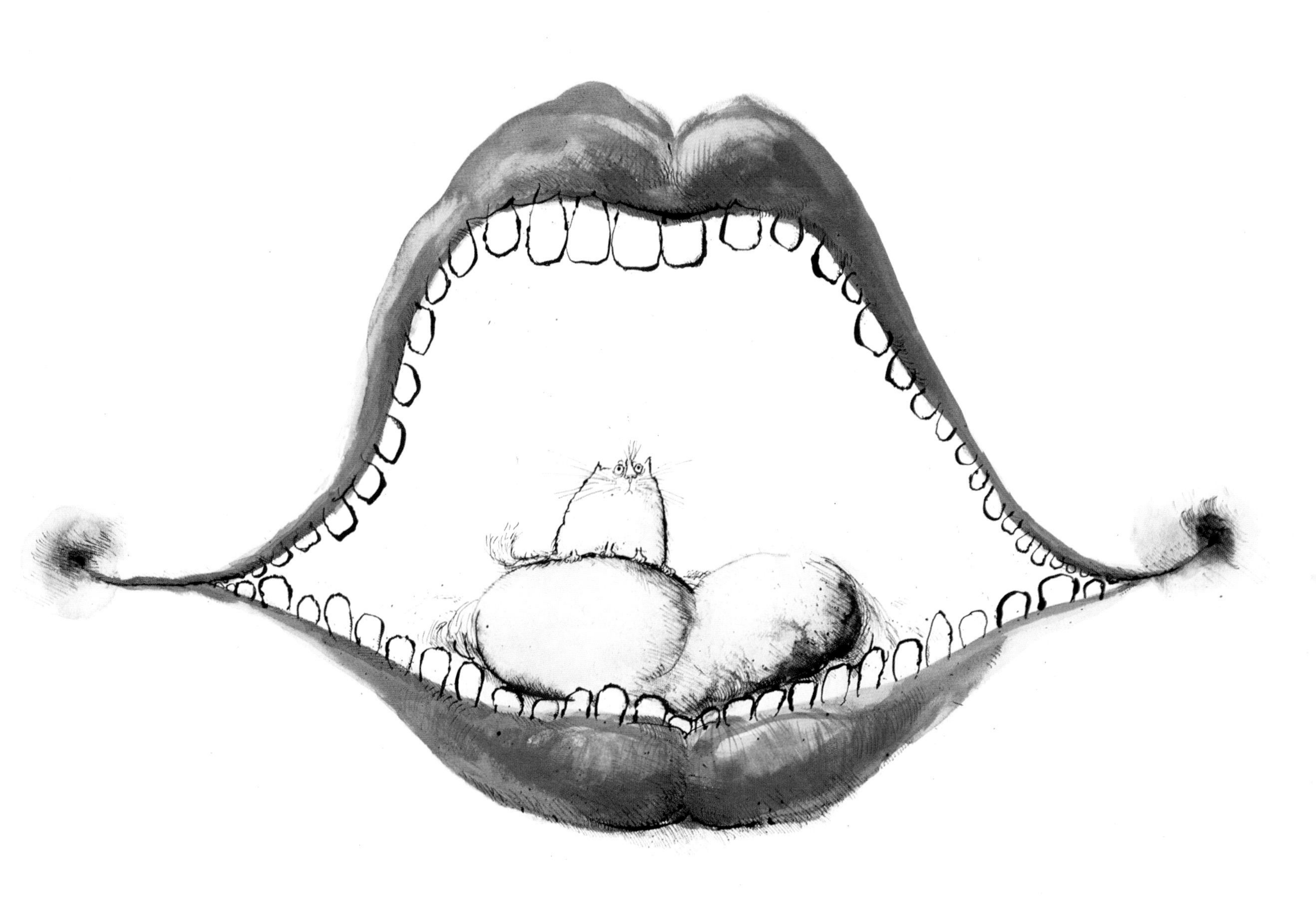

Family Man

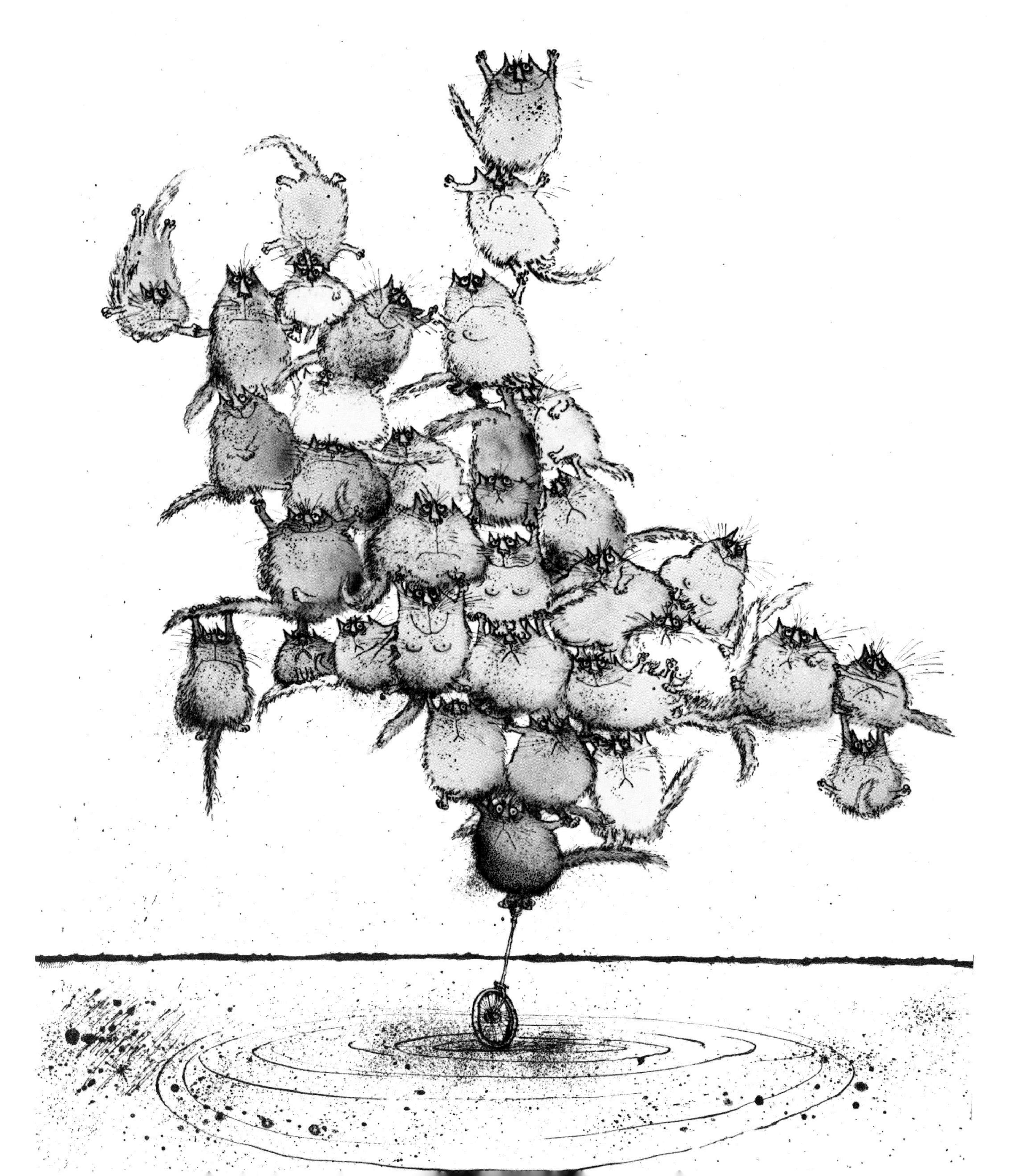

Hey! There's a cat in the garden. . .